SUPERBASE 13

WILLIAMS

SUPERBASE 13

WILLIAMS

The Quest For Silver Wings

Philip Handleman

ACKNOWLEDGEMENTS

My thanks go to the dedicated personnel who showed me how a sprawling pilot training facility like Williams Air Force Base can smoothly and efficiently accomplish its critical ongoing mission. Those people to whom I am ever so grateful include: Capt Linda Britt, Lt Rockford 'Rocky' Willett, TSgt Bob Tucker, Sgt Mike Richmond, A1C Ken Hawkins, A1C Eric Parnell, Arlene Enfield, Lori Bolerjack, Sgt Jeff Drazil, Lt Col Bill Fuller, Lt W J Morgan, SrA Alice Glick, Lt Jason Mogle, Tom McCoy, Capt Amy Brandon, Lt Bruce Desautels, Lt Paul Gates, Lt Gretchen Krueger, MSgt Nathaniel Daggs, Capt Bernard Mater, MSgt Tom Trent, A1C Christine Campbell, Lt Col Ronald Diedrichs, SSgt Nigel Beckford, Lt Andy Hurling, Sgt Eric Prothe, Sgt Tony Harris, Capt Frank Gebert, Capt Scott Chapman, Lt Col Russ Allen, Sgt Scott Diprofio, Lt Mark Mitchell, SSgt Edward Terhune, Lt Sandra Graves, Lt Col Michael Perry, Capt Kenneth Lang, SMSgt John Baker, Sgt Dennis Williams, Col Ronald Smith, Col Bernard 'Jerry' Stecklein, Lt Col John Callen, and Capt Sammie Grizzle. While I would not have been able to undertake this project without the help of everyone mentioned here, I am, of course, the one who is responsible for the content of this book.

Published in 1990 by Osprey Publishing Limited
59 Grosvenor Street, London W1X 9DA

© Phillip Handleman 1990

British Library Cataloguing in Publication Data
Handlemann, Philip
  Williams: the quest for silver wings.
  1. United States, Air force. Pilots Training
  I. Title   II. Series
  358.4'3'07

  ISBN 0-85045-962-1

Editor Tony Holmes
Page design Paul Kime
Printed in Hong Kong

Front cover With the azure blue skies forming a breathtaking backdrop, a gleaming T-38 Talon sits on the Williams ramp awaiting instructor and pupil

Back cover His bulky parachute firmly strapped to his torso, a student pilot begins the delicate job of squeezing into the small T-37 cockpit

Title pages Rows of aged but effective Cessna T-37 primary jet trainers grace the Williams Air Force Base parking ramp

Right This curvaceous North American F-86 is a reminder of Williams Air Force Base's past. In the 1950s, Sabres were used at Williams for fighter gunnery training. This pedestal-mounted example at the main entrance to the base is encircled by the colourful flags of the 50 states, indicating the presence of students from every part of the country. The aircraft is dedicated to Air Force pilots killed in Korea

To the young men and women in quest of silver wings

Introduction

Nestled in the Valley of the Sun on the southeast periphery of the expanding Phoenix metroplex is a pilot factory. Williams Air Force Base, or 'Willie' as the locals call it, is the western world's largest undergraduate pilot training facility—producing about 350 of the world's finest pilots each year.

Named after Charles Linton Williams, an Arizona-born US Army pilot who perished in a flying accident during the 1920s, Willie traces its beginnings as a training site to the summer of 1941. It seemed increasingly likely to policy planners in the Army Air Force that the war in Europe and Asia would soon engulf the US, and that incredible numbers of new pilots would be required in short order for the maximum effort to thwart the hostile foreign forces. Once the US entered World War 2, Willie personnel, with a heightened sense of urgency, began flight training even before construction was completed. Today, after having graduated over 25,000 students, that same spirit of motivation is evident everywhere at Willie.

Being at the forefront of change and innovation is a Willie specialty. A group of talented Willie pilots formed the Air Force's first jet aerobatic demonstration team using P-80 Shooting Stars. This hearty band of aerial performers continued wowing airshow audiences nationwide until a fuel shortage brought an abrupt halt to their public derring-do. The Acrojets, as they were called, set the stage for the Air Force's permanent air demonstration team, known to millions throughout the world as the Thunderbirds. In the 1940s Willie became the first Air Force base to institute jet pilot training. In 1977 Willie graduated the Air Force's first women pilots, now a common occurrence for the service.

For today's visitor, Willie's environment is at first dominated by the unbearably loud and virtually endless shrieks of the T-37 and T-38 training aircraft. As the day unfolds, the next obvious environmental factor is the oppressive heat; in summer ambient temperatures typically rise to over 100 degrees Fahrenheit. In these conditions—united by a love of aviation—ground crews, instructor pilots and students, indeed, the whole sprawling infrastructure of Williams Air Force Base, focus on the critical goal of filling Air Force cockpits with the best qualified flyers. After a gruelling one-year training programme that results in some young officers being washed out, the successful students receive their silver wings and go on to challenging flying assignments.

A contagious enthusiasm permeates Willie (as is surely the case at ATC's other undergraduate pilot training bases) for here is where bright and idealistic young officers congregate to serve their country and learn to fly. In their noble quest, the students engage in an unusual camaraderie that is refreshing to behold. As one enters through the main gate, the baggage of the everyday world is miraculously left behind and such vanishing values as loyalty and dedication are found intact and thriving. Willie is an inspiring place.

Contents

The Talon

After mastering basic aviator skills in the relatively tame T-37, Air Force student pilots move up to the Northrop T-38 Talon supersonic trainer. The Talon is a hot aeroplane, and the consensus seems to be if you can handle one of these then you can fly anything in the Air Force inventory

Left Fresh out of the washrack this sparkling T-38 glistens in the Arizona sun

Above Each T-38 gets attentive care from dedicated ground crews who go to great lengths to ensure the airworthiness of the Williams aircraft. Here a T-38's canopy gets a thorough polish

11

Left A student on one of his first hops in a Talon performs a meticulous walk-around preflight check, the standard procedure for every flight. Students who make it through the primary phase of flight training can expect to log about 109 hours in the T-38

Above Williams Air Force Base made history in 1977 when it graduated the first female pilots into the modern US Air Force. Today it is common to see not only women students but also women instructors. One of those instructors, sporting a G-suit and strapped to a forty pound parachute, climbs into the rear cockpit (the instructor's office) of a T-38

Overleaf Student and instructor communicate through intercom microphones in their respective oxygen mask assemblies. Instruments are checked for proper readouts before taxiing. The instructor in the rear cockpit is perched slightly higher to allow for improved forward visibility

Top left Once the checklist is completed and all systems are go, the T-38 taxies out of its parking spot on the huge Williams tarmac, fetching a fond wave from the aeroplane's crew chief

Bottom left The ambient midday temperatures in Arizona's Valley of the Sun, as the greater Phoenix area is known, commonly exceed 90 degrees Fahrenheit. Accordingly, the training aircraft such as this T-38 normally taxi with canopies raised. The aircraft air conditioning systems are effective only when airborne

Above Formation flying in the T-38 is an integral part of pilot training at Williams. The T-38, with two J85-GE-5 afterburning engines, is a powerful and responsive aeroplane that can climb to 30,000 feet in one minute

Here four Talons from the 97th Flying Training Squadron (FTS) rendezvous for formation practice. The usually clear desert sky is ideal for Williams flight operations

Above In formation flight, the T-38s may get as close as three feet apart in terms of their wingtip separation. The success of formation flight depends a great deal on the steadiness of the team leader and the constant alertness of the wingmen

Right The all-white Talon paint scheme, helpful for sighting during night flight, stands out against the magnificent buckskin terrain below. In the lead is the 97th FTS Commander's aeroplane, recognizable by the special tail marking that includes the squadron number, followed by aeroplanes from each of the squadron's student flights as denoted by the different colour fin stripes

The sleek and slender lines of the attractive T-38 are apparent as this four-ship formation streaks over the beautifully rugged and sharply defined landscape of the Arizona high desert

Left The T-38's underside planform view is clearly evident as this wondrous training aircraft passes overhead during a routine series of touch-and-goes on one of the three parallel runways at Williams

Above The T-38 is one of the more strikingly handsome aircraft in the Air Force inventory with its long nose, sleek fuselage, and short span wings. During a normal approach to landing, flaps are extended as is the case here

Above Shortly before the outbreak of World War 2, a barren stretch of Arizona desert was chosen as the location for Williams Air Force Base in large measure because of the desert's consistently good weather. Blue skies often frame T-38s like this one on final approach at Williams

Right Typically, on weekdays there is hardly a moment at Williams when trainers are not in the traffic patterns of the three runways. The continual flow of traffic, engaged for the most part in executing touch-and-goes, makes Williams an extremely busy air base. Here a T-38 clears the outer perimeter fence just before landing

The moment of truth! Milli-seconds before touchdown co-ordination is the key. Because the T-38 has the high minimum landing speed of 155 knots, some of the students find it difficult to control on landing. Perhaps in no other phase of the undergraduate pilot training course is so much skill required. Just the right inputs of control stick and throttle are called for in bringing the Talon back to earth. Not surprisingly, this aspect of the training course is sometimes a stumbling block for students who have made it through the preliminary hurdles in the early part of the flight programme

A T-38 at rest during an interval between training sorties

This view of the T-38 cockpit conveys a sense of the cramped quarters. The knobs atop the control stick are visible in the foreground. The bottoms of the rudder pedals can be seen below the instrument panel. On the right is a red banner attached to a safety pin that prevents inadvertent operation of an ejection device

Up close, the instrument panel presents a straightforward layout of flying gauges and engine dials. The artificial horizon in the centre and at the top of the panel dominates. The modern Air Force places substantial emphasis on instrument flight, so students have to develop proficiency flying 'under the hood'

Left Talons were first delivered to the US Air Force in 1961, the final airframe delivery taking place in 1972. Considering the age of this aircraft type and its heavy use, it is a credit to the designers and builders as well as the maintenance crews that it continues to soldier on so effectively in its demanding role. Regularly scheduled maintenance is performed on all the aircraft. Depending on the aircraft's accumulation of flight hours and its service history it may be virtually disassembled, with appropriate parts repaired or replaced, and then pieced back together

Above A key to the success of the outstanding flight safety record of these old aeroplanes at Williams is the pride the maintenance crews take in their job. Also, the various repair specialists co-operate with each other. As one mechanic in the engine shop said, 'It's a team effort.' Plans are under way, as a cost-cutting measure, to shift the aircraft maintenance responsibility from the military crews to civilian contractors

Overleaf Indicative of the high standards applied by the Williams maintenance crews is the fact that even the maintenance hangar floor is kept very clean

The General Electric J85-GE-5 afterburning engine, capable of producing 3850 pounds of thrust, is an old but reliable powerplant. Here an engine, after extensive maintenance, undergoes a sustained run up in one of the specially designed static test cells at Williams. The exhaust is vectored out of the test cell which is located in a remote section of the base. If the engine checks out, it will be re-installed in one of the training aircraft

Above The ageing T-38s are expected to remain in service as Air Force trainers through the turn of the century. What is a common sight today—T-38s lined up and waiting for their students—was a common sight nearly thirty years ago and should be still after the year 2000

Right Williams Air Force Base boasts over 100 T-38s. Seen here is a section of the T-38 parking area

U.S. AIR FORCE

WELCOME

82ND FLYING TRAINING WING

Painted on the Williams transient ramp is a 'red carpet' for visiting officers. Because of the vast distances involved, some Williams maintenance personnel commute across the flight line by bicycle. In this scene one of man's earliest forms of mechanized transportation is juxtaposed with one of the most modern forms

Cessna Tweet

Left Unlike the other Air Force Commands, Air Training Command does not have to indulge in the often drab, low-visibility paint schemes for its aircraft. This Cessna T-37 Tweet sports a bright star with striped bars as well as the new two-tone paint scheme. Halving the aircraft in two distinct colours is to assist an outside observer in determining aircraft direction and attitude

Above The helpful hand of the crew chief conveying the helmet to a student getting ready for flight

Above At first, the Tweet's instrument panel may intimidate the fledgling student pilot, but in short order the average newcomer adjusts to the Air Force flying environment and develops a reasonable comfort level in the T-37, which, after all, is a relatively simple and forgiving aeroplane to fly. Unlike the faster and generally more demanding Talon, the T-37 employs side-by-side seating so that student and instructor can see each other as well as talk to each other

Right The undergraduate flying training squadrons are divided into flights. As might be expected, each flight has adopted a specific name and symbol. Represented here is Good Grief Flight of the 96th FTS. Note the shoulder patch that employs the *Snoopy* cartoon character

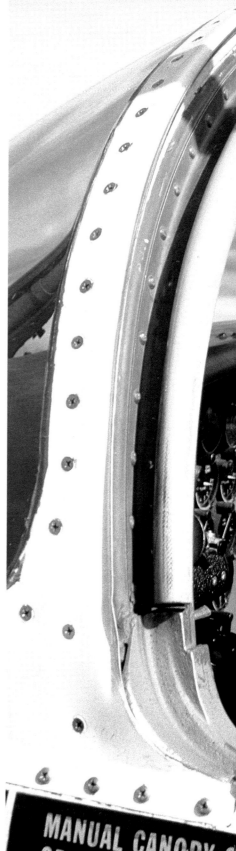

MANUAL CANOPY

Student pilots have been receiving their initial jet training on the Tweet since the sturdy little T-37 entered service in 1957

Above As a T-38 taxies past in the background, the Tweet's flight crew gets ready for taxi in what has become a busy cockpit. The crew chief stands by with hearing protectors, ready to combat the screeching whine of the T-37's engines. With the incessant high-pitched screeching of the Tweets' J69 engines and loud whine of the Talons' J85-GE-5 engines, the Williams flight line noise level is incredible. The sound never lets up during weekdays and hearing protection is a must

Right The clam-shell canopy is a distinctive feature of the T-37 which was designed expressly for primary flight training. Students average about 87 hours of flight time in the T-37

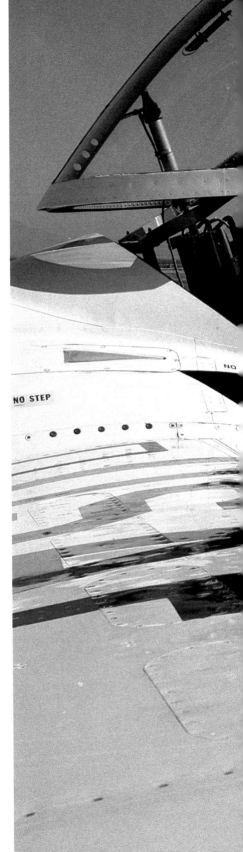

Left Despite all the high tech in the Air Force of today, communications between T-37 flight crew and crew chief are reduced to hand signals when those unbearably loud J69s start. The classic thumbs up is still very much in use, its meaning still the same: all is go

Above The T-37 is slow for a jet aeroplane. Its two ancient Continental J69 engines each produce only 1025 pounds of thrust

Above left A true workhorse in Air Training Command, the T-37 has remained in service and has contributed to the pilot training effort longer than anyone imagined it would when it made its first flight in 1955. Mastering the basic skills for take-off and landing are among the first steps in the primary flight training syllabus. Here a T-37 shoots touch-and-goes at nearby Coolidge Municipal Airport, an airport used to handle the overflow traffic from the saturated Williams airspace

Below left Aerobatics are part of the introduction to Air Force flying. The T-37 is taken out to designated practice areas at specified altitudes for a full series of basic aerobatic manoeuvres from loops to spins. This part of the flight training programme contributes to safety and builds piloting skill and confidence. The demands on Air Force student pilots make them, upon graduation, among the best in the world. However, learning to fly can be fun. As one student pilot at Williams remarked, 'Aerobatics is our reward'

Above Against the omnipresent Santan Mountains, one more T-37 in a never-ending procession flares just prior to landing. In the distance is a T-38, perhaps an incentive to the T-37 students, for after successful completion in the primary phase they move up to the fighter-like Talon

Above Not all tasks associated with flying at Williams Air Force Base are glamorous. Every inch of a weary Tweet gets a thorough cleaning in the washrack

Above right Keeping these old aeroplanes airworthy long past their originally intended service lives entails keeping them clean. A special cleansing solution is sprayed on using a high pressure hose. The cleaning crew, which rotates periodically to maintain morale, dons protective clothing. The Tweet's big brother, the Talon, occupies the adjoining berth in this washrack

Below right The Williams crews that toil away in oppressive heat at these less than glamorous jobs day in and day out keeping the trainers ready for flight are among the Air Force's unsung heroes

The T-37's durability is aptly described by a Williams maintenance technician.
'It is a tank', he declared, referring to Tweets in general. Here a starboard
engine is being removed for inspection as part of the established maintenance
programme. The engine removal can be accomplished in about half an hour

Each year a small number of foreign students from allied nations come to Williams to receive their undergraduate pilot training. Moreover, the T-37 has been employed as a trainer over the years by many foreign air forces

Above As Williams Air Force Base operates 91 Tweets, the parking ramp is filled with T-37s

Right The side-by-side seating arrangement makes for an especially effective primary flight training environment. The eye contact between student and instructor that this seating arrangement provides is quite valuable

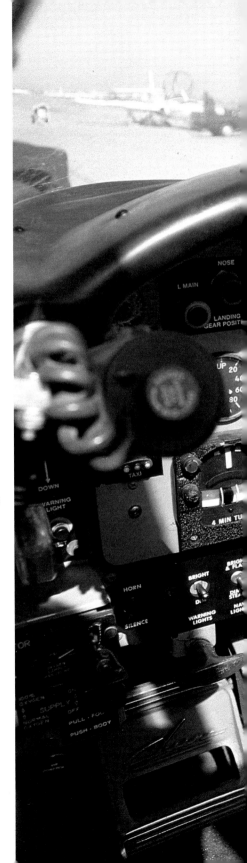

Williams graduates approximately 350 students as Air Force pilots each year. This makes Williams not only the largest undergraduate pilot training facility in the Air Force, but also in the western world. The base's reputation for excellence, the appealing climate, and the proximity to a major urban centre make a Williams assignment very desirable. A T-37 bakes under the bright Arizona sun

Basic training

Right Before getting their hands on the controls of an aeroplane, the student pilots are subjected to the rigours of life support training. Here a pilot trainee is dragged over a field by his classmates to simulate the effects of an open parachute canopy pulling him across the ground after an ejection. He is taught to manipulate releases on his harness to free himself. Each student gets a few such rides, both face up and face down

Above Though the student pilots are not required to make either an ejection or a parachute jump, they are trained for that eventuality should an emergency require such action. Here students jump off a platform to practice the proper impact absorbing techniques associated with a parachute landing

Left A more sophisticated simulation of a parachute landing is created through the use of this scaffolding device. Instructors from the base's aerospace physiology unit are on hand to teach the students proper procedures

Above The preflight training continues at the old Rittenhouse Auxiliary Air Field which is a short drive from Williams. Here the students are given further schooling in life support techniques. The class is being instructed in the use of the equipment in the standard issue Air Force pilot's survival kit. The instructor is about to activate a high intensity flare which is why many of the students are shielding their eyes

Above The culmination of the day's life support training is the series of three parasail rides per student. Each student is towed by an Air Force pickup truck until a sufficient altitude is obtained. At just the right moment, the cable is released and the student floats down under the parasail, simulating a parachute fall

Right The truck races across a sandy field once used as a runway, kicking up a cloud of dust as the parasail lifts a student pilot

Above A student pilot's first flight at Williams Air Force Base is this rather docile parasail ride. The tow line is visible as the trainee hams it up during his ride by waving to his classmates below

Right When the inquisitive groundcrew arrives in the drop zone, the student pilot, no matter how hard the landing, invariably responds that it was a fun ride and that he is just fine. The attitude of the student pilots is uniformly gung-ho, and at this early stage in their training programme they are not about to let a bruise or bump dampen their spirits

A student pilot awaits his launch

Above left Shortly after impact, each member of the class receives a succinct, mild-mannered but firm critique from the wise and watchful Master Sergeant Nathaniel Daggs. The knowledge, dedication and skill of experienced enlisted personnel like MSgt Daggs keep the Air Force training programme at Williams and the other ATC bases working at a level near perfection. The concern and professionalism of MSgt Daggs and his aerospace physiology colleagues scrambling along the dusty landscape of Rittenhouse may years later save the lives of some of these young would-be pilots

Below left An eager student pilot getting strapped into the parasail harness for his first ascent at Williams Air Force Base

Above Among aviator rituals is the customary dunking of a student pilot upon completion of his first solo flight. Like their predecessors, these young officers gleefully toss their newly soloed classmate into the water. Because of the volume of the Williams flight training activity, the dunking tank remains filled to the rim

Above All Air Force student pilots must be commissioned officers and virtually all are college graduates. The academic portion of the training programme is in its own way as demanding as the flying training. As can be seen here, the standard uniform even in the classroom is a flight suit

Above right In one of the study halls, a wall mural depicts a simulated dogfight between an aggressor F-5 and an F-15 air superiority fighter. When it comes to requesting future assignments, many student pilots express a preference for fighters

Below right Students train together. Here two student pilots from the 99th FTS's Tipper Flight, with their distinctive Bunny shoulder patches, review their flight plan

Above Weather briefings are a standard part of flight planning at Williams

Above right The daily flight schedule for T-37s is posted on the board at the supervisor of flying desk in the headquarters building for the 96th and 98th FTSs. This system makes it easy to keep track of equipment and personnel

Below right The supervisor of flying desk on the T-38 side of the base serves the same purpose. Here flight crews are preparing to sign out aircraft for their training sorties

Left Last stop before the flight line is a check of the oxygen mask in a life support unit

Above Safety officer of the Devil Cats of the 97th Flying Training Squadron is Captain Scott Chapman. Among the more experienced instructor pilots, Capt Chapman was previously asssigned to Strategic Air Command as a B-52 pilot

Recognition and Graduation

Above As part of the day's formal retreat, the *National Anthem* is played and the flag is lowered. Later, at the ceremony's conclusion, the folded flag is presented to the retiring MSgt Hernandez in recognition of his years of devoted service

The Air Force pays tribute to those special people who devote a large part of their lives in selfless service to their country. One late afternoon as the day's activities wound down at Williams, an eclectic group of onlookers formed on the grassy area in front of base headquarters. In a moving ceremony, Master Sergeant Jose Hernandez officially retired after serving over twenty years in Air Force maintenance and engineering. MSgt Hernandez is seen at attention on the right as the honour guard takes position

Right The 21 graduates of Williams class 89-05, like more than 25,000 Williams students before them, were presented their hard-earned silver wings. The 'pinning' ceremony is an informal affair, calling on parents or spouses to do the honours

Above The 52-week pilot training experience ends on this happy note for those highly motivated young officers with the tenacity and talent to stick with the programme. In addition to their shiny wings, the newly graduated pilot's carry with them their first assignments as Air Force pilots. Whether it is on to SAC, TAC, MAC or back to ATC, these bright young pilots, beaming with boundless enthusiasm, ultimately are the Air Force's future

Left On graduation day parents can hardly help bubbling with pride over the accomplishment of their son or daughter. An instructor pilot of one of the graduates told his former pupil within earshot of the graduate's parents, 'I'd fly with you any day'

Above Before long the dress blue uniforms will give way to sage green flight suits and these new Air Force pilots will engage in their chosen profession of flying

Base tour

Left Set in the Arizona desert, the campus-like grounds of Williams Air Force Base include an impressive cluster of tall palm trees just inside the main gate

Above Among the base's static displays is this sun-drenched Lockheed P-80 Shooting Star, the Air Force's first operational jet fighter. These types were used for training at Williams following World War 2, giving Williams the distinction of being the Air Force's first jet pilot training base. Significantly, in 1946 Lieutenant Colonel Bob Worley led a group of flying compatriots using P-80s based at Williams, in the markings shown here, in a newly formed team called the Acrojets—the US Air Force's first jet air demonstration team and a forerunner to the now universally acclaimed Air Force Thunderbirds. The Acrojet pilots were a loosely organized group that just liked to perform aerobatics, and continued at shows around the country until a fuel shortage brought a premature end to the team

Above A snappy salute is likely to greet any authorized visitor to Williams Air Force Base — the largest undergraduate pilot training facility in the western world

Right In the adjacent town of Higley, the major thoroughfare leading to the base's main gate is appropriately designated Williams Field Road

Left The nearby community of Chandler is home to this F-86 monument

In conjunction with each active runway at Williams is a remote supervisory unit staffed by at least one instructor pilot and several student pilots. The RSU personnel maintain continuous radio communication with aircraft in the landing pattern, ensure proper separation and flow of traffic, and visually check that each approaching aircraft's landing gear and flaps are functioning. This RSU is located at Coolidge Municipal Airport, which relieves the heavy Williams traffic load

Above Here RSU personnel have cleared a Tweet for landing, and watch it during roll out

Right The scope of the sprawling Williams complex is evident from the vantage point of the control tower. These young airmen have a great view and considerable responsibility

Above Always on alert, the flight line fire crew is prepared to move into action at a moment's notice. While the aged training aircraft fleet causes many alarms to be sounded, fortunately few are serious emergencies

Right Line maintenance is divided into sections. Here the so-called Apache unit stands ready as a T-38 taxies past

425
Deputy Commander
Operations
Instrument Flight
Simulator
International Training

This impressive structure, tastefully landscaped with native cacti, houses both the T-37 and T-38 high tech flight simulators. Located elsewhere on base is the Air Force Human Resources Laboratory's Operations Training Division which is engaged in the development of even more sophisticated flight simulators

Above An old Link Trainer, symbolizing early efforts in flight simulation, occupies space in the open stairwell of the flight simulator building

Right A student and instructor are riding this modern flight simulator through the 'rough air' generated by a computer. The unit's massive legs move briskly at the computer's commands, producing a realistic sense of motion for the officers enclosed in the imitation cockpits above

Badges of honour

Above The 97th Flying Training Squadron is divided into four flights, one of which is called Skitter. The officers of Skitter Flight proudly wear their shoulder patch that sports a design of two T-38s in formation streaming fire from the dual exhausts and set against a partial checkerboard scheme. The unique shoulder patch designs help to instill an esprit de corps which the Air Force hopes its student pilots will maintain through their myriad career assignments

Right Each class passing through Williams designs its own shoulder patch. The artwork is amazingly creative. In a particularly colourful example that in mural form now decorates a wall in a squadron building, the sixth class of 1980 concocted the improbable scene of a Talon hurtling over the planet amid the stars in space. The patch's words of wisdom, now emblazoned on the wall, advise today's students 'ON SOLO NO ONE CAN HEAR YOU SCREAM'

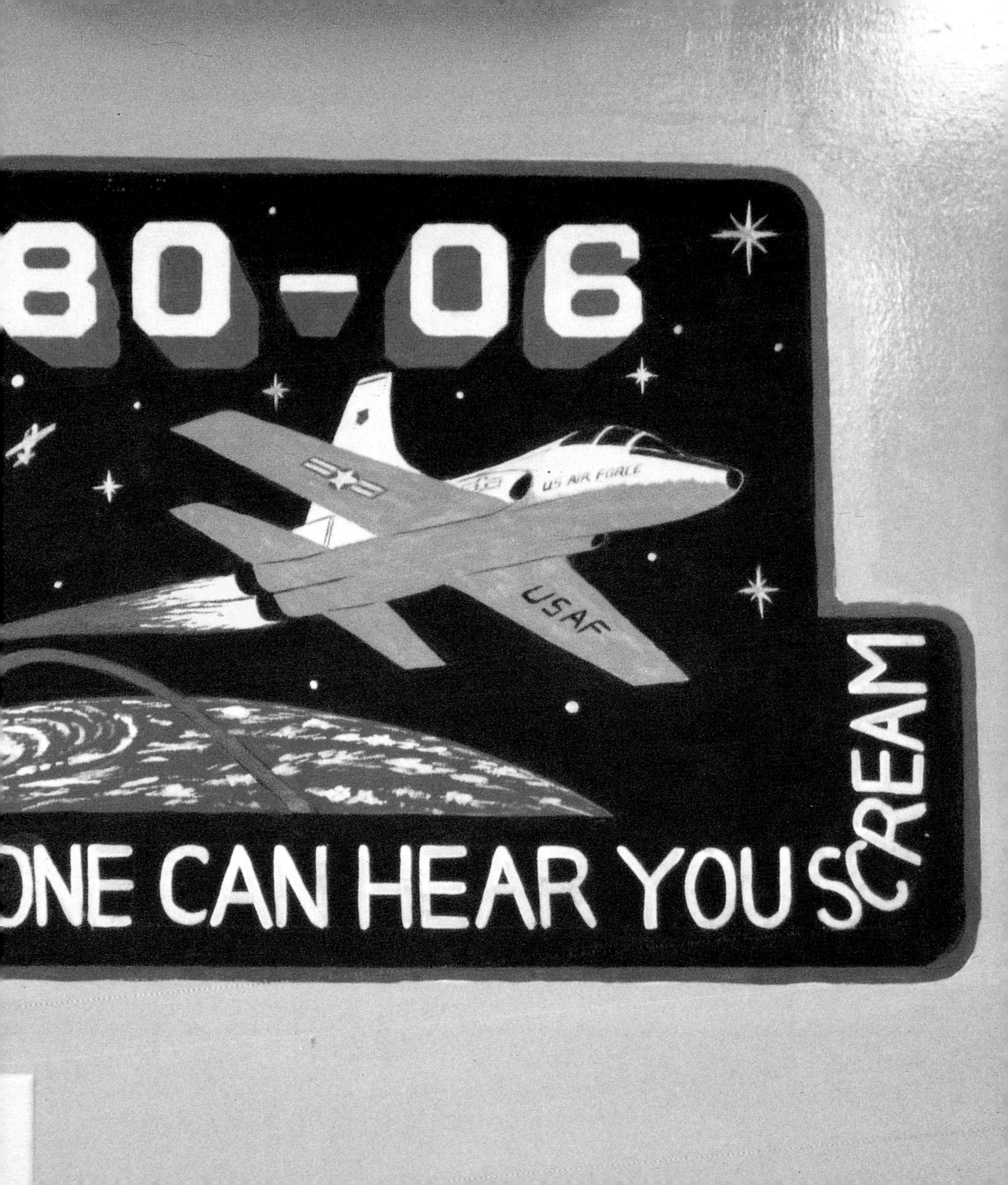
80-06
US AIR FORCE
USAF
ONE CAN HEAR YOU SCREAM

Air Training Command's emblem appropriately symbolizes learning with a lighted torch

The 82nd Flying Training Wing traces its roots to the 82nd Fighter Group which repeatedly distinguished itself during World War 2. On 10 June 1944, the 82nd, flying twin-engined P-38 Lightnings, conducted the longest and one of the most hazardous fighter-bomber missions of the Mediterranean campaign. Half of the aeroplanes that reached the target, the Ploesti oil fields in Rumania, did not return. Against incredible odds that resulted in a heavy cost, the 82nd's Lightnings inflicted substantial damage on the target. For this action, the 82nd received its third Distinguished Unit Citation. Although redesignated a training wing in June 1972, and activated as such in February 1973, the 82nd retains its illustrious history—its emblem, now frequently in the company of cactus plants as shown here, a reminder of that history

Left The squadron emblems shown here decorate the exteriors of the two squadron buildings—one dedicated to T-37s (housing the 96th and the 98th) and the other to T-38s (housing the 97th and the 99th). Each of the four squadrons that today comprise the 82nd Flying Training Wing has its own distinct history. It is noteworthy that the 99th Flying Training Squadron's predecessor, the 99th Pursuit Squadron, opened a remarkable chapter in Air Force history when in March 1941 it became the first Army Air Force unit in which blacks could pilot military aircraft. In the face of enforced segregation, the 99th Pursuit Squadron accumulated a brilliant combat record, its members fighting for freedom abroad while being denied equality at home. The old 99th's emblem of a golden orange winged panther in striking position has been adopted by the 99th Flying Training Squadron. The history behind this emblem serves as a source of continuing inspiration

Above By custom, each incoming class paints one of the rocks in front of the base headquarters building. Here a class has chosen the charming Charles Schulz comic strip character *Snoopy*, which is often associated with aviation, as a sign of their presence on base. Upon the class's graduation a different paint scheme produced by yet another incoming class will decorate this rock. And so the tradition at Williams carries on

Tiger II

While Williams is known as an undergraduate pilot training base, it has played host to the 425th Tactical Fighter Training Squadron since 1964. The 425th provides advanced fighter training to pilots of allied nations and has used the Northrop F-5E Tiger II for this purpose. Here, four F-5s are shown in a relatively low formation pass

Above This Tiger II approaches the active runway as a primary flight student practices a touch-and-go in a T-37

Left The 425th is assigned to Luke Air Force Base's 405th Tactical Fighter Training Wing, but the 425th's F-5s have been based at Williams because of the maintenance commonality between F-5s and T-38s. This is understandable since both aircraft types stem from the same manufacturer, Northrop Corporation. The Tiger II's general appearance resembles that of the Talon, but the F-5E is a single-seater with more powerful J85-GE-21 engines that produce 5000 pounds of thrust each

Left Dummy bombs for practice
bombing runs await installation

Above The fierce head of a growling
tiger adorns the tail of a Tiger II. The
relative low cost, simplicity, ease of
maintenance, and good performance
characteristics have made the F-5E a
popular export item. In excess of 1000
Tiger IIs have been delivered to 19
nations

In 1989, the 425th is scheduled to convert to the F-16, reflecting the upgrading of many allied nations to newer fighter aircraft. At the time of conversion the 425th will relocate to Luke Air Force Base on the opposite side of Phoenix

'Willie Day'

For one weekend each year Williams Air Force Base invites the public to an open house called Willie Day, the 1989 event featuring the crack US Navy air demonstration team, the Blue Angels. The team's sleek F/A-18 Hornets lined up on the transient parking ramp in front of the permanent 'red carpet' for VIP visitors

A couple of days preceding the base's formal open house, the Blue Angels performed a full practice routine which constituted a private airshow for base personnel lucky enough to be unoccupied at the time. Normal protocol calls for the base's senior officer to greet the team members upon landing after their practice routine. With all other flight operations at Williams cancelled for the day, the Commander of the 82nd Flying Training Wing, Colonel Jerry Stecklein (on the left), extends a hearty pilot's welcome to the six performing members of the Blue Angels team

During an unusually quiet moment at Williams, Col Stecklein (centre) confers
with some of the Blue Angels pilots

Above A Blue Angels team member hands out descriptive brochures to awe-struck children

Right An exceedingly popular attraction wherever they perform, the Blue Angels pilots are typically surrounded by affectionate autograph-seekers at airshows across the country. Here team leader, Commander Pat Moneymaker, prepares to accommodate a crowd of admirers during Willie Day

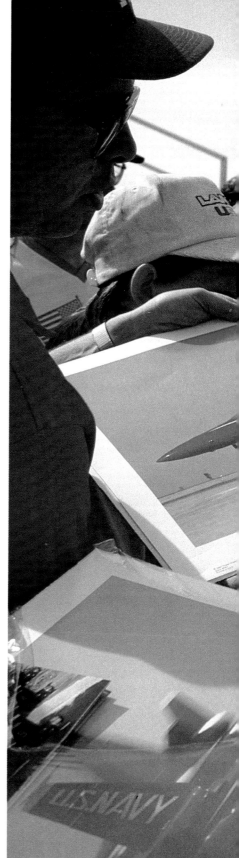

Above left The Blue Angels fly the McDonnell Douglas F/A-18 Hornet, an amazing aircraft that has both fighter and attack capabilities. Its naval aviation orientation is evident in the beefed up landing gear that must be able to withstand the repetitive shock of carrier landings

Below left Although the maintenance crews receive only a tiny share of the public's attention, their contribution to the team's success is invaluable. Here maintenance crewmen tend to the unglamorous but nevertheless important details. Because of this superb maintenance the Blue Angels have never had to cancel a scheduled appearance due to technical malfunctions

Above The Blue Angels during their warm-up, like the student pilots on a normal day at Williams, are reduced to the old method of communication by hand signals

Left The famed Blue Angels six-ship delta formation graces the cloudless sky over Williams Air Force Base in the Arizona desert

Above As one of the six aircraft splits off to perform solo manoeuvres, the remaining five Hornets climb line abreast ever so precisely

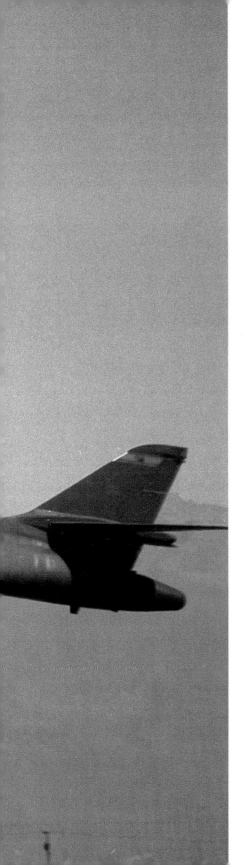

Left Among the impressive displays at Willie Day '89 was the Rockwell B-1B bomber, shown here silhouetted against the Superstition Mountains upon arrival

Above With less than one hundred in the Air Force inventory, the awesome B-1B is an often sought but rarely obtained airshow aircraft. Williams was fortunate to secure one for its open house

Below The first stop for Williams graduates assigned to fighters is likely to be Holloman Air Force Base in New Mexico where they will receive fighter lead-in training in the AT-38B, a modified version of Northrop's dependable Talon. Note the glossy blue camouflage paint scheme of this Holloman-based B model on display during Willie Day

Above Possible future Air Force pilots stepping up to the cockpit of a Williams T-38 for a look inside. The annual Williams Air Force Base open house not only affords taxpayers from the surrounding communities an opportunity to see their tax dollars at work but allows young people like those pictured here to learn more about military aviation

Right Some of the more enterprising sorts from the base set up a scale T-38 model in the bicentennial Air Force Thunderbirds air demonstration team colours along the static display line during Willie Day. The poster beckons 'GET YOUR PICTURE TAKEN IN AN AIR FORCE MINI-JET!' Many children, smitten by the aviation bug, could be seen tugging on trouser legs and skirts for the chance to sit in the trainer mockup and indulge supersonic dreams